THERE AR̶
GRASSLANDS
IN MY BACKYARD!

By Walter LaPlante

Gareth Stevens
PUBLISHING

Please visit our website, www.garethstevens.com. For a free color catalog of all our high-quality books, call toll free 1-800-542-2595 or fax 1-877-542-2596.

Library of Congress Cataloging-in-Publication Data

Names: LaPlante, Walter, author.
Title: There are grasslands in my backyard! / Walter LaPlante.
Description: New York : Gareth Stevens Publishing, [2017] | Series: Backyard biomes | Includes bibliiographical references and index.
Identifiers: LCCN 2016025782| ISBN 9781482455519 (pbk.) | ISBN 9781482455533 (library bound) | ISBN 9781482455526 (6 pack)
Subjects: LCSH: Grassland ecology–Juvenile literature. | Lawn ecology–Juvenile literature. | Urban ecology (Biology)–Juvenile literature.
Classification: LCC QH541.5.P7 L38 2017 | DDC 578.75/54–dc23
LC record available at https://lccn.loc.gov/2016025782

Published in 2017 by
Gareth Stevens Publishing
111 East 14th Street, Suite 349
New York, NY 10003

Copyright © 2017 Gareth Stevens Publishing

Designer: Andrea Davison-Bartolotta and Bethany Perl
Editor: Kristen Nelson

Photo credits: Cover, p. 1 robert cicchetti/Shutterstock.com; pp. 2–24 (background texture) wongwean/Shutterstock.com; p. 5 Wolfgang Kaehler/LightRocket/Getty Images; p. 7 JaySi/Shutterstock.com; p. 9 (vicuna) Dirk Ercken/Shutterstock.com; p. 9 (map of South America) Bardocz Peter/Shutterstock.com; p. 11 Oleg Znamenskiy/Shutterstock.com; p. 13 Auscape/Universal Images Group/Getty Images; p. 15 Wild Horizon/Universal Images Group/Getty Images; p. 17 (giraffe) Pyty/Shutterstock.com; p. 17 (zebra) Ehrman Photographic/Shutterstock.com; p. 17 (lion) Keith Levit/Shutterstock.com; p.17 (elephant) Donovan van Staden/Shutterstock.com; p. 19 Barcroft Media/Getty Images; p. 21 Volodymyr Burdiak/Shutterstock.com.

Printed in the United States of America

CPSIA compliance information: Batch #CW17GS: For further information contact Gareth Stevens, New York, New York at 1-800-542-2595.

CONTENTS

Boldface words appear in the glossary.

Out Your Window

When you look outside, do you see a lot of grass and few trees? You might live on grasslands! This **biome** may be found in the middle of **continents** or near the ocean. North America, South America, Asia, Africa, and Australia all have grasslands.

Grasslands are a biome that gets enough rain every year for many kinds of grasses to grow. There isn't enough rain for many trees to grow, though. The trees that do grow on grasslands are small, thin, and far apart.

Kinds of Grasslands

Temperate grasslands have hot summers. Rain in the early spring and summer helps the grasses grow. The grasses are often short and soft. Grasses don't grow during winter because it can be very cold.

South America

Pampas

Tropical grasslands, or savannas, are hot all year. They get more rain than temperate grasslands, but also have a time of year when little rain falls. Tropical grasslands have very tall grasses. Some grow to 6 feet (1.8 m) tall!

Dry Times

Grasslands have dry periods called droughts. It may get so dry that the grasses catch fire! Trees often can't **survive** the drought and fire. Grasses, though, can keep growing below ground even if they're burned above ground!

What Lives There?

The grasses you see in grasslands depend on where you live. On temperate grasslands, you might see buffalo grass, purple needlegrass, and galleta. These grasslands often have flowers, too, such as asters, sunflowers, and coneflowers.

sunflower

15

On North American grasslands, bison, wolves, coyotes, and prairie dogs are just some of the animals you might spot. Tropical grasslands in Africa are home to giraffes, zebras, lions, and elephants. Imagine seeing one of these animals in your backyard!

zebra

lion

elephant

giraffe

17

Biome Balance

All living things on grasslands need each other. As grasses grow, **grazing** animals eat them. These animals become food for predators. Too many or too few of any plant or animal would upset this **food chain**.

19

People like to build and plant crops on grasslands. Too many people living on grasslands take homes away from animals, though. People's water use and **pollution** harms the biome, too. If you have grasslands in your backyard, take care of them!

GLOSSARY

biome: a natural community of plants and animals, such as a forest or desert

continent: one of Earth's seven great landmasses

food chain: the order of living things in a biome in which each uses the next lower member as food

grazing: having to do with feeding by eating grasses and crops

pollution: trash or other matter that can harm an area

survive: to live through something

temperate: having a mild climate that's not too hot or too cold

tropical: having to do with the warm parts of Earth near the equator

FOR MORE INFORMATION

BOOKS

Higgins, Melissa. *Grassland Ecosystems*. Minneapolis, MN: Core Library, 2016.

Waxman, Laura Hamilton. *Life in a Grassland*. Minneapolis, MN: Bellwether Media, 2016.

WEBSITES

Grassland
kids.nceas.ucsb.edu/biomes/grassland.html
Learn the different words used for grasslands around the world and other facts about this biome.

Grassland Animals
mbgnet.net/sets/grasslnd/animals/
Read more about the many animals that live on grasslands around the world.

INDEX